WHY DO COCKATIELS DO THAT?

Real Answers to the Curious Things Cockatiels Do

By Nikki Moustaki
Illustrations by Buck Jones

BOWTIE PRESS®

IRVINE, CALIFORNIA

Ruth Strother, Project Manager
Nick Clemente, Special Consultant
Michelle Martinez, Editor
Karla Austin, Associate Editor
Michael Vincent Capozzi, Designer

The birds in this book are referred to as *he* and *she* in alternating chapters.

Library of Congress Cataloging-in-Publication Data

Moustaki, Nikki, 1970-
  Why do cockatiels do that? : real answers to the curious things
cockatiels do / by Nikki Moustaki ; illustrations by Buck Jones.
     p. cm.
  ISBN 1-889540-96-X (pbk. : alk. paper)
  1. Cockatiel--Miscellanea. I. Title.
  SF473.C6 M65 2003
  636.6'8656--dc21
                                        2002010706

BowTie Press®
A Division of BowTie Inc.
3 Burroughs
Irvine, California 92618
949-855-8822

Printed and Bound in Singapore
10 9 8 7 6 5 4 3

For my parents who indulged me in birds

—N. M.

For Kim, Satchel, and Riley

—B. J.

Contents

Why Do Cockatiels Desire Constant Attention?

Cockatiels, who are part of the parrot family, are among the many species of birds who live in flocks that range from a few birds to hundreds. Flocking is one of the cockatiel's natural defenses against predators—there's safety in numbers.

A flock also alleviates loneliness. Cockatiels are social animals who rely on their flockmates for company, mutual preening, finding a mate, and so on. But what's a cockatiel to do when he's a lone bird in a human household? Fortunately, the cockatiel is an adaptable animal. Instead of searching endlessly for other cockatiels, the companion cockatiel comes to regard his human companions as part of his flock. And not

only do human flock members provide security and company but they provide food and water as well.

You might notice that your cockatiel calls for you tirelessly when you leave the room. He wants to know where his flock members have gone. Are they safe? Are they coming back? Perhaps your bird vocalizes loudly when he sees a predator such as a hawk in the sky or the neighbor's cat in the yard. Your cockatiel is telling you to beware—there's danger lurking. Essentially, the companion cockatiel has the same drive as his wild relatives do to preserve the integrity of the flock. Aren't you glad to know that your cockatiel is watching out for you?

Why Do Cockatiels Come in So Many Colors and Patterns?

Popular birds such as cockatiels, lovebirds, and budgies, who have been bred in captivity for hundreds of years, are often available in many colors. Many of these colors are mutations. Occasionally, a member of a species is born (or in this case, hatched) with different physical characteristics than the rest of the species. For example, take the wild male cockatiel. He's a gray bird with yellow cheeks and an orange face patch. That's it. Not yellow, not white, no fancy pearling on the feathers. Gray is a good color for the cockatiel, a bird who is considered a snack for predators in the outback.

So, how did the cockatiel come to be available in so many

wonderful colors? Well, every now and then, under just the right conditions and with just the right gene pool, a bird breeder (called an aviculturist) will find a baby in the nest box who looks far different from the others. This baby is visually carry-

ing the genes for a color different from her parents. The aviculturist will then breed that bird, hoping that the gene will pass on visually. If it doesn't, no problem—the genes have still been passed along to some of the babies, even if they don't show up visually. These genes are likely to appear in the next generation or the next.

Basically, humans take a rare, natural occurrence and capitalize on it, creating birds who wouldn't naturally be found in such numbers in the wild. This practice is widely accepted in the bird community, and is the reason for the multitudes of colors found in many popular bird species today.

Is Your Cockatiel a Boy or a Girl?

Determining the sex of your cockatiel is easy if your bird is the normal gray color and has come into mature feather, around eight to twelve months of age. The male develops bright yellow cheeks and a bright orange face patch; females have the same coloring, but it is far more muted. Mature females also have a barring pattern on the underside of their tail feathers, and males do not. In most of the cockatiel's mutations, this barring pattern is an indication that the cockatiel is female. Males can have barring before their first molt, so be careful to take this into consideration. In the pretty pearl mutation, most males lose the pearling and retain the base color, therefore, a strongly pearled adult cockatiel is a hen.

Lutinos (yellow birds) present more of a problem if they are very light in color—you have to look closely to see the barring. Some very light or white cockatiels cannot be correctly sexed visually. You can take the bird to your avian veterinarian for DNA sexing if you absolutely must know. And, of course, if any bird lays an egg, she's a female—no question!

Why Do Cockatiels Have a Head Crest?

Unlike a feather in a cap, the crest on top of a male and female cockatiel's head isn't there for decoration. The crest plays an important role in cockatiel body language. It helps a cockatiel express himself and is considered by many owners to be a great interpreter of mood and attitude.

When a cockatiel is resting, content, and just going about his business, the crest should be flat on his head with just the tip arching upward. The cockatiel raises the crest to full height when playing exuberantly or when he is surprised, excited, or frightened. When the crest is plastered flat to the cockatiel's head and the bird is hissing, spitting, and has his beak open, watch your fingers! This bird is feeling defensive.

The crest is the cockatiel's way of telling the world how he's feel-ing at the moment. There are many varia-tions to the bear-ing of the crest, and you'll come to know how your individual cockatiel reacts to different stimuli by watching the position of the crest. Cockatiel owners are lucky to have an additional way to determine their birds' moods.

Why Do Cockatiels Grind Their Beaks?

Do you ever hear a tiny gritch, gritch, gritch sound coming from your cockatiel's cage? Some novice cockatiel owners are alarmed by the sound of grinding beaks, but actually this is a normal, healthy behavior. No one is certain why parrots grind their beaks, but it is known that the behavior is *not* similar to teeth grinding in people, which indicates stress. Beak grinding reflects contentedness and a relaxed state. Most cockatiels grind their beaks just before falling asleep or when they are resting deeply.

Some people believe that the grinding has something to do with keeping the beak trim, but there's no evidence to prove

or disprove that hypothesis. So, if you hear the little gritch, gritch, gritch of your bird grinding her beak before a nap or just before bedtime, you can be assured that your bird is comfortable and feeling well. Ill birds generally drop the beak-grinding activity until they're feeling better.

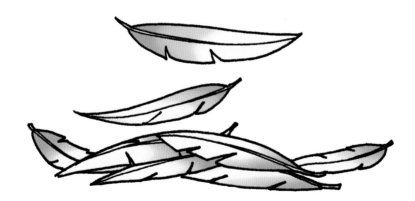

Why Do Cockatiels Regurgitate to a Significant Other?

When a cockatiel, generally a male, forms a bond with another cockatiel, a human companion, or even a beloved toy, he may offer his beloved a mouthful of predigested food as a token of affection. What a *charming* animal, you might be thinking. Yeah, right. But, if you were a bird, you'd be honored by such a gesture! Bonded birds regurgitate to each other and to their babies, both to preserve the bond between the pair and to offer predigested food to youngsters who can't eat on their own yet.

A regurgitating cockatiel pumps his head and neck a few times (to upchuck his lunch) and then stretches out his head to

offer a mouthful of half-digested material. But don't worry—rarely does the regurgitated material fly out of the beak. The bird usually gives the stuff only to someone willing to take it. If your cockatiel is courting you with regurgitation behavior, you can be assured that you are the sun and the moon of his birdie life. Take the honor—but not the gift!

If you notice regurgitated material on your cockatiel's face or chest or if you believe that your cockatiel is ill because he is regurgitating excessively, take him to your avian veterinarian right away. You may discover that your bird simply has a case of lovesickness, but you'll want to make sure he's not actually ill.

Why Do Cockatiels Produce So Much Dust?

Have you ever dusted near your cockatiel's cage, only to find the next day it looks like you haven't picked up a dust rag in months? Cockatiels, cockatoos, and African grey parrots are notorious dust producers. People with allergies should consider another type of bird, or at least buy a good air purifier. Neatniks need not apply.

The fine white dust comes from the powder-down feathers that grow closest to a cockatiel's skin. This powder serves to keep the feathers waterproofed and clean. The only way to keep the dust in check—not eliminate it—is regular bathing and misting with clean, tepid water several times a week.

Always allow your bird to be well dried before going to bed, so only bathe her in the daytime and in warm weather.

The dust that your cockatiel produces may make you sneeze, and it may make your cockatiel sneeze as well. This is normal. Unless you notice discharge from your bird's nostrils or other signs of illness, don't worry too much about the little *achoos*. Never, ever try to remove anything from your cockatiel's nose—there's a hard plate in the nostril that's supposed to be there. Some owners try to take it out. Ouch!

Why Do Cockatiels Often Whistle Better than They Talk?

Well, the simple answer to this is that whistling is easier to learn than talking. The cockatiel is not known to be the most proficient talker in the parrot world, although some individuals learn to talk quite well. Cockatiels may like whistling more than talking because whistling is closer to birdsong, especially for the male, who uses song for courtship. Male cockatiels are reputed to talk more frequently and more clearly than females, but there are exceptions. Some believe that if you teach a cockatiel to whistle before you teach him to talk, he will never talk. This is generally untrue. He just may whistle *more* than talk.

Teaching Your Cockatiel to Talk and Whistle

If you want a cockatiel who's going to be vocal, start with your choice of bird. Watch a group of cockatiels and choose the one who's making the most racket—that's a bird who likes to vocalize.

Teaching a bird anything is all about repetition. Once you decide what you want your cockatiel to learn to say, simply repeat it over and over as clearly as possible. It's important to sound excited and enthusiastic when you say the word or phrase because birds are attracted to energy; the more energy you put into what you're trying to teach your bird, the faster he will learn. This is why birds learn "no!" "be quiet!" and curse words way too easily!

Why Do Cockatiels Become Seed Junkies?

Does your cockatiel gorge herself on seed, even though there's a full dish of fresh fruit and veggies right in front of her face? It's not just because seed is fun to eat (though it is!) or because your bird is used to eating seed, though that's part of it. In the wild, cockatiels feast on young grass seeds as long as they are available, usually when water is plentiful. These young seeds are full of nutrients, and, best of all, full of calories, which wild cockatiels need in abundance when they nest and breed. As long as seeds are available, which accounts for only a few months a year (unless there's a farm growing grain nearby), wild cockatiels eat them.

Your companion cockatiel has the same programming. If there are seeds available, well, you can fill in the rest. But, dry seeds don't have the nutritional value that young seeds and sprouts do, which means that the "seed-addicted" cockatiel is getting a lot of calories without the same amount of nutrition. Ultimately, this can lead to a fat cockatiel with liver problems, fatty tumors, and gout.

This isn't to say that seeds are bad—they are good for your bird when served in moderation as a part of the total diet, which should include veggies; fruit; specially cooked birdie foods; pellets; and safe, healthy table foods.

Food Tips for Your Cockatiel

- The best veggies and fruits to feed your cockatiel are dark green or dark orange in color.
- Make sure you wash all produce thoroughly before offering it to your bird.
- Never feed your cockatiel alcohol, chocolate, or caffeine, each of which can be deadly.
- Part of the avocado pit is toxic to birds, so avoid avocado too.
- Raw rhubarb isn't recommended.
- Raw onions and tomatoes aren't toxic, your cockatiel just won't like them!

- Seeds in any fruit or veggies, except melons and squashes, can be toxic, so take them out before feeding these items to your bird.
- Cockatiels do not need the supplement grit, and can even die if they gorge on it.
- Cockatiels will appreciate a cuttlebone and mineral block in the cage.
- If you offer your bird chicken eggs, which are high in nutrition, boil them for at least thirty minutes to avoid any avian diseases that may have come with the egg.

Why Do Cockatiels Vocalize Persistently?

The cockatiel is one of those birds we wish came with a mute button. This is a bird who vocalizes consistently throughout the day, whether by whistling, calling, singing, talking, squawking, squeaking, peeping, or any other number of sounds. Cockatiels are not *loud* birds, comparatively, but they are not quiet either. Sunrise (or when the bird wakes up) and dusk are particularly noisy times. In the wild, cockatiels vocalize loudly at these times, so it's natural that your cockatiel does the same.

There are periods of quiet during the day when the cockatiel is eating, napping, or playing on his own. But other than

that, a cockatiel is generally engaged in some sort of vocalization activity. Contact calling, when your bird calls you repeatedly to make sure you're okay and that he's not alone, can be loud and persistent. Simply call back and tell your cockatiel you're fine (not kidding here) and see if that helps.

If your cockatiel is making a giant racket, something might be wrong with him. Check to see if there's something in the area that's agitating the bird or if a toe is caught in the cage or a toy. Perhaps your female is calling for a mate, or your male is singing his best, and loudest, courting song. Whatever the reason, no matter what you do, you're not going to live with a silent cockatiel. Love the noise or buy some earplugs!

Why Do Cockatiels Become Afraid of the Dark?

The phenomenon of night frights or night thrashing isn't exclusive to cockatiels, but it seems to happen to cockatiels more often than to any other companion bird. Cockatiels become fearful in the dark and launch themselves against the sides of the cage, often breaking feathers and injuring legs, feet, and eyes. This loud nighttime thrashing is frightening for the cockatiel owner too.

The most likely cause of night frights is something unknown and unseen entering the cockatiel's space. It could be a mouse scurrying across the floor, the family cat sneaking around in the dark, or something moving near or outside a window, such as shifting curtains, a tree limb brushing against the glass, or the glinting light from a car. A family member sneaking a midnight snack could also be to blame.

If your cockatiel is thrashing, simply turn on the light and speak softly to her. Do not try to remove her from the cage immediately, but you do need to inspect the bird for injury at some point. The best way of dealing with night frights is to prevent them. An inexpensive nightlight that is automatically activated in the dark should do the trick.

Why Do Cockatiels Sleep on One Foot?

Most healthy cockatiels sleep with one leg pulled up and out of sight, which may look uncomfortable but is actually a bird's way of keeping cozy while he sleeps. Both a bird's body temperature and the ambient temperature drops at night so it makes sense for the bird to draw a foot into a warmer part of the body during sleep. A bird who's maintaining the proper body temperature doesn't have to work so hard to metabolize food and preserve energy. Because a cockatiel's legs are a site of heat loss, the bird conserves heat by placing one leg where it's warmest, among the feathers of the stomach.

A cockatiel who's sleeping on two feet is cause for concern. Keep an eye on this bird—he may not be feeling well. If you notice that your cockatiel is sleeping on both feet, feathers puffed, eyes droopy, or has any other symptoms of illness, take him to the avian veterinarian right away.

Why Do Cockatiels Preen Themselves (and One Another—or You!)?

Because they feel pretty, oh so pretty! Preening is the act of cleaning and aligning the feathers. It is a normal behavior for a healthy cockatiel. To you, it might look like your cockatiel is bothering her feathers, or picking nits—don't worry—she's just going through her daily grooming regimen.

To understand why cockatiels preen, you first have to understand how feathers work. Feathers are unique to birds as a family and are probably the most important structure on a wild bird's body. A wild cockatiel could not survive for one day without feathers! Companion cockatiels can function well without certain feathers, but certainly not without all of them.

On the whole, feathers are extremely important to a bird's existence.

Feathers regulate body temperature and, of course, allow for flight. To function correctly, a bird's feathers must be clean, dry, and in good shape, not ragged or torn. Each feather is made up of many strands that fasten together kind of like a zipper. During preening, a cockatiel makes sure that each feather is zipped up properly. A cockatiel runs her beak over each and every feather on her body, every single day—with the exception of the feathers on the top of her head and at the back of her neck, which she relies on her mate or buddy (you) to reach.

A cockatiel also has a gland at the base of her tail that secretes oil used to keep the feathers supple and waterproof. The cockatiel picks up some of this oil with her beak and runs it though her feathers. This is an important part of a healthy cockatiel's daily routine.

Mutual preening, or allopreening, is also a normal event in the daily life of a cockatiel living in a pair or group. Allopreening functions both to reinforce the bond between two birds and to ensure that feathers in unreachable places get preened too. A cockatiel living alone doesn't have the benefit of allopreening and will want you to understudy as a bird and learn how to preen. It's pretty simple. A human-bonded cockatiel who's comfortable with you and her environment will put her head down and offer you her neck as an invitation for preening. Scratch her head and neck lightly, ruffling the feathers, not smoothing them down. Be gentle and preen only the head and neck unless your cockatiel indicates that you can proceed farther.

To a cockatiel, hair is the human equivalent to feathers. You might find that your bird likes to preen your hair, eyebrows, mustache, or beard. This is quite endearing and shows that your cockatiel trusts you and considers you worth her interest.

Why Do Cockatiels Lose Their Feathers?

A cockatiel molts once or twice a year, losing feathers from all parts of his body. Make sure you have your handheld vacuum on hand during your bird's molt, because you will be surprised at how many feathers one little cockatiel can lose! Molting is normal, though, and is nothing to become alarmed about unless you see bald patches (with the exception of the bald patch behind the crest in some lutino cockatiels). If you do see bald patches, take your bird to an avian veterinarian right away.

Your cockatiel is extrasensitive during a molt and may become snappish or want to stay in his cage. At the very least, he may not behave like his normal, perky self. This is because your cockatiel is growing new feathers, which takes a lot of energy. Your cockatiel is simply tired. Also, the feathers that are growing in tend to be itchy and the process is sometimes painful, so your cockatiel may just want to chill out and not be bothered for a while. Don't fret, though, the molt will be over in a few weeks to a few months, and your bird will be back to normal.

New feathers are enclosed by thin, whitish sheathes made of keratin, the same material that composes our fingernails. Your cockatiel spends a lot of time opening these sheathes to let the new feathers emerge more easily. He might need help with the feathers on top of the head, so if you and your cockatiel are great friends, gently crush the sheathes with a clean fingernail when your bird offers you his head for preening. Remember, these sheathes can be painful and the feathers inside of them have a blood supply, so move as slowly and gently as possible. Lightly misting your cockatiel with clean, tepid water also helps to soften these sheathes and makes feather growth a little less irritating.

Molting Cockatiel Cake Crumble

Feed your cockatiel extra protein during a molt. Hard-boiled eggs, sprouted beans, and pieces of chicken are good sources of protein. Feed dark green and orange veggies and fruits in abundance as well—carrots, kale, cantaloupe, and cooked squash are good choices. Here's a recipe that molting cockatiels will appreciate. You can offer this food all year long too.

1 package corn muffin mix

1 egg (as indicated on muffin package), including shell

¼ cup spinach, chopped (fresh or frozen)

¼ cup fresh carrots, grated

¼ cup beans, any type, sprouted or from a can (not dry)

¼ cup mixed dried fruit

¼ cup small bird pellets, organic

2 teaspoons calcium powder (optional)

Mix the corn muffin mix according to the package. If the package calls for an egg, use the whole egg, including the crushed shell. If it does not call for an egg, hard-boil an egg, crush it, and add it along with the rest of the ingredients. Once the mix is blended, add the other ingredients and stir well. Bake in a greased cake pan according to the directions on the package, allowing extra time for the other ingredients to bake—it may take twice as long as indicated. When a knife comes out of the center clean, cool the cake on a wire rack. Crumble it into large chunks and freeze. Thaw a portion each day and offer it to your cockatiel.

Why Do Cockatiels Fluff Their Feathers?

Feathers are fabulous temperature regulators. Why do you think down beds and coats are so popular? A cockatiel's fluffed-up feathers trap heat close to her body by locking air inside the spaces between the feathers. The feathers and the trapped warm air preserve the bird's body temperature by not allowing cooler air to get to her skin.

Being fluffy is okay when a cockatiel is sleeping at night, but it isn't a normal continuous state for a cockatiel. If your bird is fluffed up for a long period of time, try to asses what could be causing her to want to retain heat. Is the bird's environment too cold? If yes, make the room warmer (but not

with a space heater, which can emanate fumes that may be harmful to your bird).

Sometimes, when a bird feels ill, she tries to keep her body temperature high by remaining fluffed. If you notice that your cockatiel is fluffy and sleepy during hours when she should be awake and perky, consult your avian veterinarian.

Cockatiels also do a quick tension-releasing ruffle fluffle of the whole body after preening that helps to get rid of trapped debris in the feathers. A cockatiel who's feeling threatened or defensive may puff up to seem large and menacing. This kind of feather fluffing is usually accompanied by other behaviors such as hissing and biting.

Why Do Cockatiels Poop So Often?

This one is easy: so you have to clean more often! Actually, there are two reasons your bird might leave presents on your T-shirt several times a day. First, cockatiels, like all parrots, poop often so they can fly. Birds need to be streamlined and as light as possible for flight, which is why some of their bones are hollow. A bird who's holding in a load of poop is a heavier bird who has to work harder to fly. This is why nature has given birds, such as cockatiels, a very small place in their bodies to hold poop, forcing them to eliminate far more often than most other animals.

Secondly, cockatiels, like many of the smaller parrots, have a high metabolic rate. This means that they have to eat a lot to

maintain their body weight and to keep everything working the way it should. So, if a cockatiel eats often, he will poop often. Now, how to get cockatiel poop out of the new white carpet . . .

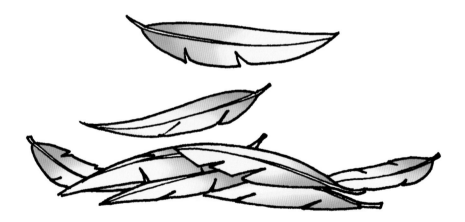

Why Do Cockatiels Like to Sit in High Places?

The better to see you, my dear. Cockatiels do many things simply because they're prey animals. Though wild cockatiels feed on the ground most of the time, they are especially alert and would rather be up in a tall tree surveying the landscape for other animals who would eat them.

Your curtain rods, ceiling fans, and chandeliers all make fabulous yet dangerous perching places for a cockatiel. A ceiling fan is especially dangerous, and chandeliers may contain toxic metals. If you don't want to have to retrieve your beloved pet from high in the rafters, consider clipping her wings or offering her a safer place to fly.

Some people theorize that allowing a bird to sit higher than your head makes her feel superior to you. This may be true for individual birds, but on the whole, a well-socialized cockatiel should not be discouraged from sitting in a high spot at times. She feels *safe* up there! To make you both happier, try hanging a playgym where your bird can watch the world to her little birdie heart's content.

Why Do Cockatiels Destroy Antiques (and Sofas, Drapes, and Rare Books)?

Part of the unexpected that comprises cockatiel ownership is finding that your cockatiel prefers to gnaw on your priceless Picasso rather than on his wooden bird toys. To a cockatiel, your expensive antiques seem like a bounty of destructible material, and he will have a chew-fest the moment you turn your back. But don't worry—your cockatiel isn't a snob—he will destroy inexpensive furniture too. Fortunately, the cockatiel has one of the smaller beaks in the hookbill family, so the damage is not as great as it could be with a larger parrot.

Cockatiels in the wild have a lot to do; they have full-time

58

"jobs." They forage for food, search for water, build nests, and raise their young. Your cockatiel lives a much different life. He doesn't need to expend nearly the amount of energy that his wild relatives do, yet he's still compelled to live as they live. This is part of the reason it's so important that a cockatiel is allowed to chew on safe items.

Providing your cockatiel with plenty of chewable toys and perches—and not becoming angry with him when he chews them into toothpicks—will help keep him occupied and away from other items. Of course, the best way to keep your cockatiel away from your antiques is to supervise closely during out-of-cage playtime.

Chewing also provides your cockatiel with much-needed exercise and can offer mental stimulation in an otherwise dull day. Let your cockatiel chew—just not on your prized possessions!

Toy Tips for Your Cockatiel

To keep your cockatiel entertained (and away from your furniture), rotate toys in and out of the cage on a weekly basis. This makes each toy seem new and interesting. It also allows you to clean and disinfect the toys you've just removed by using a 10 percent bleach solution and rinsing well in hot water. Remember to keep your bird's favorite toy inside the cage at all times—occasionally a toy can substitute for a friend or mate, and you don't want to take your cockatiel's "buddy" away unless the bird's behavior becomes problematic.

You can't put a stop to destructive behavior, but you can make sure that your cockatiel's energies are directed to the proper items. Provide your bird with a wide variety of toys in a variety of materials:

- soft wood
- sisal rope
- leather
- lava rock
- hard plastic
- acrylic

Why Do Cockatiels Bite Sometimes (or All the Time!)?

Has your sweet little cockatiel become a biter? Even though the cockatiel has a small beak, a properly placed bite can still hurt! Birds bite when they feel threatened or afraid. It's that simple. Birds perceive situations differently than we do. What might seem fine to you, such as sticking a hand into a cage, might be seen by the bird as an affront—after all, that cage is the cockatiel's home. Another example: your precious hen, who has never bitten you before, has laid an egg and now she's vicious. Of course! She's protecting her young (well, her preyoung), and she sees your hand as a threat. You can almost always diagnose biting this way.

One bite may have stemmed from your cockatiel feeling threatened, but continuous biting is a learned behavior. Here's the scenario: Your cockatiel, for whatever reason, has bitten you. You reacted by screaming, jumping around, and running for a Band-Aid. Such power your bird has over you! The bird has just learned a valuable lesson: *If I bite, the threat goes away and I'm treated to a fabulous show of my owner screaming and jumping, which I love.* So, what are you going to do when you get bitten? Nothing. Just walk away and ignore your cockatiel for a few minutes. Your bird can't imagine a worse fate than being ignored by her flockmates. When your bird has calmed down, resume your interaction.

Why Do Cockatiels Hate the Family Cat and Dog?

Cockatiels are prey, and dogs and cats, no matter how cute and fluffy they seem, are predators. Imagine living in a home with a mountain lion and a grizzly bear roaming around the place. It wouldn't make for a relaxed atmosphere, would it?

No matter how much you train your dog or cat to stay away from your cockatiel, you can never eliminate the instinct to kill small, fast-moving things. What kind of dog do you have? It is important to remember that spaniels and retrievers are bred to hunt birds, terriers are bred to kill vermin and small animals, and sight hounds are bred to kill small, fast-moving things. Isn't your cockatiel a small, gray, scuttling object? Where does that leave your bird?

Cats—forget it. You'd have a better chance trusting Jack Sprat's wife at a fat-eating contest. Unless your cat is blind and deaf and has only two legs, don't chance losing your bird. Cats have bacteria on their teeth and claws that are so deadly to birds that one small scratch can kill a bird within twenty-four hours. If your dog or cat even so much as touches your cockatiel, take the bird to the avian veterinarian right away. Keep Kitty and Fido away from your cockatiel—even the best trained pets will, at the very least, frighten your bird if they get too close.

Why Do Cockatiels Lay Eggs, Even Without a Mate?

Cockatiels have been called the rabbits of the bird world, and for good reason. A mature cockatiel hen wants to breed, and she starts laying eggs with or without a male. Just like chickens, cockatiel hens can lay infertile eggs. This is normal, but it's not always healthy. A few eggs a few times a year are okay. But when a hen lays continually, calcium and other important elements are not replenished in her body quickly enough, causing her bones to become brittle and her eggs to become soft. This can lead to egg binding, a sometimes deadly condition.

If your cockatiel hen is laying eggs and has decided to sit on them, let her play mom until she abandons them, which will be in about three to four weeks, when she realizes they aren't going to hatch. If you keep taking the eggs away as soon as she lays them, she will keep laying. Some cockatiels lay eggs from a perch. These eggs usually break at the bottom of the cage. You can remove broken eggs because your bird won't be interested in them anyway.

Feed a laying hen extra calcium sources such as green vegetables, and make sure she has a cuttlebone in her cage. A shot of calcium from an avian veterinarian is also recommended.

To prevent a hen from continual egg laying, expose her to only eight to ten hours of light a day, using either a cage cover or a darkened room. This simulates wintertime, when wild cockatiels don't breed because there isn't enough food and water. Her hormones will take a break and she should stop laying. If she doesn't stop laying, take her to your avian

veterinarian. It might seem like a natural thing for a cockatiel to lay enough eggs for a giant omelet, but it's not healthy for her. Besides, you can get your eggs at the grocery store!

Nikki Moustaki has worked in aviculture and bird rescue and rehabilitation since 1988. She writes regularly about birds for *Bird Talk* magazine, *Birds USA*, and *Pet Product News*. Nikki also owns and hosts Birdy Works at www.birdyworks.com, a site dedicated to the care and training of companion birds. She is the author of several books about bird care and training, including two other books on the subject of cockatiels and *Why Do Parakeets Do That?*

Buck Jones's humorous illustrations have appeared in numerous magazines (including *Dog Fancy* and *Cat Fancy*) and books. He is the illustrator for the best-selling books *Barking*, *Chewing*, *Digging*, *House-Training*, *Kittens! Why Do They Do What They Do?*, *Puppies! Why Do They Do What They Do?*, and *Why Do Parakeets Do That?*

For more authoritative and fun facts about birds, including health-care advice, behavior tips, and insights into the special joys and overcoming the unique problems of bird ownership, go to your local pet shop, bookstore, or newsstand and pick up your copy of *Bird Talk* magazine today.

BowTie Press is a division of BowTie Inc., which is the world's largest publisher of pet magazines. For further information on your favorite pets, look for *Dog Fancy*, *Dogs USA*, *Cat Fancy*, *Cats USA*, *Horse Illustrated*, *Reptiles*, *Aquarium Fish*, *Rabbits*, *Ferrets USA*, and many more.